Dublin is a master of
seen its fare share c
pick itself up,

Right now, north and south of the River Liffey, a wave of new cafés, restaurants and cultural spaces is reviving forgotten corners of the city. From the brunch spots of Portobello, to the towering "Silicon Docklands" and the pop-up art galleries of Stoneybatter, all signs say Dublin is on the up once more.

Best of all, the city's compact size means you can easily stroll from one neighborhood to the other. Ireland's dynamic capital promises plenty to write home about, whether you catch a performance by the next big musician or street artist, or sip on a Guinness while reflecting on the host of literary greats who walked this city's streets. There's no time like the present to go and explore.

## fiona hilliard
writer

Fiona Hilliard is a travel writer and blogger, and third-generation Dubliner. She grew up on the outskirts of the capital, where she studied journalism and media before a serious case of wanderlust took her on adventures from Mexico City to Milan and many places in between, which she chronicles on her blog, traveledits.com. When not on her travels, Fiona's love of music, fashion and cute cafés sees her exploring Dublin's hot spots one neighborhood at a time.

## Joe Ladrigan
photographer

Joe Ladrigan is an international travel photographer currently based in Dublin. To see more of his personal work, check out his Instagram @Joe.ire.

**Where to Lay your Weary Head**          5

## THE LIBERTIES                          10–19

Adonis Flower Designers                   12
Anonymous Vintage Antiques                13
Image & Ink Social Hub                    14
Mannings Bakery                           15
Teeling Whiskey Distillery                16
The Glamour Pit                           18
The Riddler Café and Restaurant           19

**But First, Coffee**                     20

## DUBLIN 7 HIBSBORO, SMITHFIELD, STONEYBATTER   22–31

Arran Street East                         24
Cotto                                     25
Dice Bar                                  26
Dublin Vintage Factory                    27
L. Mulligan Grocer                        28
Lighthouse Cinema                         29
Lilliput Stores                           30
Moo Market                                31

**Café Society**                          32

## THE QUAYS                              34–47

Bagots Hutton                             36
Bison Bar                                 37
Brother Hubbard North                     38
Cut & Sew                                 40
PÓG                                       41
Theatre Upstairs                          42
The Bakehouse                             43
The Clockwork Door                        44
The Winding Stair                         45
The Wooden Mills                          46
Yamamori Sushi                            47

**Culture Vulture**                       48

## TEMPLE BAR 50–61

April and the Bear 52
DiFontaine's Pizza 53
Find 54
Folkster 56
Indigo & Cloth 57
Roberta's 58
Rosa Madre 59
Siopaella 60
The Gutter Bookshop 61

**Ió Market** **62**

## CREATIVE QUARTER 64–75

Appassionata Flowers 66
Article 67
Cocoa Atelier 68
Designist 69
Fallon and Byrne 70
Industry & Co. 71
Om Diva 72
San Lorenzo's 73
Skinfull Affairs 74
Ukiyo 75

**Tea Time** **76**

## CAMDEN QUARTER PORTOBELLO 78–89

Against the Grain 80
Christy Bird Antiques 81
Delahunt 82
John Gunn Camera Shop 83
Las Tapas de Lola 84
Nowhere 85
Sova Food Vegan Butcher 86
The Bernard Shaw 88
The Bretzel Bakery and Café 89

**Dublin After Dark:**
Craft Cocktails — **90**
Sounds of the City — **93**

## GRAFTON QUARTER — 96–103

DesignYard — 98
Dolce Siciliy — 99
Mary's Bar and Hardware — 100
Rhinestones — 101
Sheridan's Cheesemongers — 102
The International Bar — 103

## GEORGIAN DUBLIN — 104–113

Alchemy Juice Co. — 106
CoCu — 107
Etto — 108
HotAir — 109
MAKESHOP — 110
Sweny's Joycean Pharmacy — 111
The Sugar Club — 112
Toners — 113

**Literary Pubs** — **114**

## DOCKLANDS — 116–124

herbstreet — 118
Juniors — 119
Offbeat Donut Co. — 120
Science Gallery — 122
Surf Dock Watersports — 123
The Bath Pub — 124
The Old Spot — 125

**Parks and Gardens Galore** — **126**

# CLIFF TOWNHOUSE

*Georgian gem*

22 St Stephen's Green (near Kildare Street; Georgian Dublin)
+353 1 638 3939 / theclifftownhouse.com
Double from €165

Sweet dreams are made of good food and Georgian charm, not to mention spectacular views of St Stephen's Green. At Cliff Townhouse, guests can look forward to snuggling up in one of nine sumptuous bedrooms that all come equipped with Nespresso machines and complimentary WiFi. Below, in the hotel's restaurant, blue and silver interiors evoke a casual elegance. For a taste of the local grub, try their surf and turf menu, in particular seafood specialties such as Galway oysters, Dublin Bay prawn and "posh" fish and chips made with battered cod and beautifully presented with grilled lemon. Later, head to Urchin, their basement bar for light bites and expertly mixed nightcaps.

## KELLY'S HOTEL

*Location, location, location*

36 South Great George's Street (near Fade Street; Creative Quarter)
+353 1 648 0010 / kellysdublin.com
Double from €109

Sandwiched between two lively bars, Kelly's Hotel is the ideal base for exploring the vibrant Creative Quarter. Pared-back interiors composed of queen-sized beds, white walls and wood floors give the 16 bedrooms a clean, minimalist look. The casual, in-house Candle Bar is the perfect spot to enjoy a coffee or set up office for an hour or so, and after dark, it's just a hop, skip and a jump to the neighboring pubs. Come morning, complimentary breakfast at the hotel's L'Geuleton restaurant is one very good reason to drag yourself out of bed.

## NUMBER 31

*Hosts with the most*

31 Leeson Close (near Fitzwilliam Place; Georgian Dublin)
+353 1 676 5011 / number31.ie
Double from €220

If the walls in Number 31 could talk, they'd certainly have some stories to tell. Irish architect Sam Stephenson designed this classical Georgian townhouse and modernist mews as his home in the 1950s; dinner parties here were the stuff of legend, with artists, celebrities and writers gathering in its chic sunken lounge to sip Martinis and put the world to rights. These days, the house has lost none of its aesthetic appeal. Proprietors Noel and Deirdre take great care to ensure that the 21 en-suite bedrooms are furnished to the highest standard, and go the extra mile to create a warm, welcoming atmosphere in the house and garden. Breakfast is no exception. It's included with your stay, so you can look forward to a feast of homemade breads and jams, as well as Number 31's delicious take on the full Irish breakfast: bacon, sausage, egg, tomato and potato cake.

# THE DEAN HOTEL

*Instagrammers dream*

33 Harcourt Street (near Stable Lane; Camden Quarter)
+353 1 607 8110 / deandublin.ie
Double from €150

Rich mahogany interiors. A cozy back-lit bar. Tracey Emin's neon "I Fell in Love Here" wall art.  You know you're in for a treat as soon as you set foot in the The Dean's lobby. The stylish welcome extends to the 52 rooms, which are kitted out with Marshall amps, ready and waiting for you to connect your iPhone and gadgets as well as vinyl turntables and Netflix-ready TVs. Located in the heart of Harcourt Street, one of Dublin's liveliest nightlife districts, guests are never more than a stone's throw from the city's most popular late-night bars and clubs. But you don't even have to go that far to join the party. Sophie's, The Dean's rooftop restaurant and bar also happens to be one of the city's hottest nightspots. Pack your dancing shoes.

THE DEAN HOTEL

## THE GIBSON HOTEL
*Encore!*

Point Village, East Wall Road (near Castleforbes Road; Docklands)
+353 1 681 5000 / thegibsonhotel.ie
Double from €114

Located in the Point Village, right opposite the 3 Arena,
The Gibson Hotel channels more than a little of the rock 'n'
roll swagger of its neighboring concert venue. Taking its name
from the hemidemisemiquaver music note (try saying that
three times fast), the hip, in-house Hemi Bar is the ideal spot
to raise a glass before tucking into locally sourced eats at the
ever-buzzy Coda restaurant. Rooms, in contrast, are all about
that other R 'n' R. Calm and restful, guests can expect comfy
beds, spectacular views of Dublin Port or a private courtyard,
as well as complimentary organic products — just about
everything a jet-setting rockstar could want in an
urban retreat.

THE MARKER HOTEL

## THE MARKER HOTEL

*Docklands delight*

Grand Canal Square (near Forbes Street; Docklands)
+353 1 687 5100 / themarkerhoteldublin.com

Double from €415

Sleek and sophisticated, the luxurious Marker Hotel shines like a multi-faceted jewel amidst the skyscrapers of the Docklands. Inside, room interiors are cool and minimalist, featuring statement furnishings by Philippe Starck and tranquil color schemes inspired by the Irish countryside. The chill vibes continue in the hotel's spa and wellness center, where an impressive infinity pool awaits. But the pampering doesn't end there. On Sunday afternoons, The Marker's Brasserie restaurant goes all out with its mouthwatering Le Drunch menu. Think Bloody Marys, huevos rancheros, hefty rib-eye steaks and freshly blitzed smoothies. The cherry on top? In the summer months, the roof terrace, with its panoramic views of the city, is the ultimate place to sink a cheeky sundowner.

# the liberties

Filled with market stalls, dry wit and the faint, comforting smell of roasted malt, the Liberties is one of Dublin's oldest, and most eclectic neighborhoods. As the home of the Guinness Brewery and Storehouse, the National College of Art and Design and several of the city's most historic churches, The Liberties is a vibrant jumble of activity where centuries-old tradition meets bright creative sparks. Strolling around, you're as likely to spot innovative art and design stores such as Jam Art Factory as you are to see (and hear) local grannies selling oranges and Toblerones on their market stalls. The history of the area goes back 800 years, with the name referring to a number of "free" jurisdictions that existed outside the city walls of Viking and Medieval Dublin. While linked to the city, they retained their own authority and administration. In some ways, The Liberties still hangs on to this independent spirit with its village-within-a-city feel, colorful street life and strong sense of community. Follow me and you'll see what I mean.

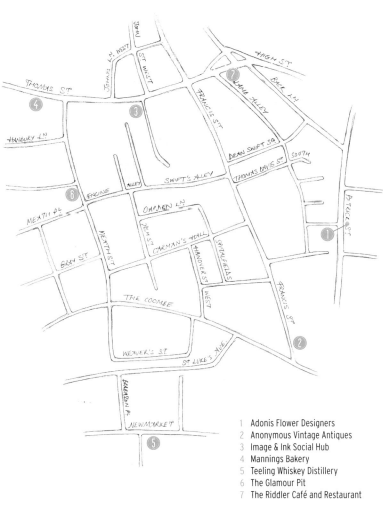

1 Adonis Flower Designers
2 Anonymous Vintage Antiques
3 Image & Ink Social Hub
4 Mannings Bakery
5 Teeling Whiskey Distillery
6 The Glamour Pit
7 The Riddler Café and Restaurant

# ADONIS FLOWER DESIGNERS

*Bloomin' marvelous*

**59-60 Patrick Street (near Bull Alley Street) / +353 1 454 5973**
**adonis.ie / Closed Sunday**

Adonis Flower Designers is no ordinary florist. Run by the flame-haired Kat, the team here specializes in unique creations inspired by all things wild and beautiful. Inside, the shop is a fragrant wonderland of exotic, freckled orchids, imaginative displays and hand-tied bouquets that look as if they've been plucked fresh from a country garden. Oh, and if you're looking to send a last-minute thank you, congratulations or to simply brighten up someone's day, the great news is that they offer a same-day delivery service.

# ANONYMOUS VINTAGE ANTIQUES

*A trip down memory lane*

**72 Francis Street (near The Coombe)** / **+353 83 325 5742**
**facebook.com/Anonymous** / **Closed Sunday**

Francis Street is to Dublin as Portobello Road is to London. This area is a little treasure trove for vintage lovers, with antique dealers, pre-loved furniture stores and secondhand charity shops lining both sides of the street. At No. 72, you'll find Anonymous packed with unique mid-century finds, from 1960s sideboards to kitschy wall art, retro pinball machines and old rotary dial telephones. If you're in any way nostalgic, this is a brilliant shop to browse. Special mention goes to their random (but completely covetable) collection of retired fairground lights. Roll up, roll up!

# IMAGE & INK SOCIAL HUB

*One-stop body art shop*

63-64 Thomas Street (near West John Street) / +353 1 531 4239
imageandink.ie / Open daily

Situated on the well-trodden path that leads to the Guinness Storehouse, this one-stop shop for tattoos, body piercings and haircuts has seduced many a visitor with their dot work, neo-traditional and mandala designs. If you haven't got the time or the nerve to commit to a permanent souvenir, the least you can do is walk away with a cup of their incredible coffee. The lovely coffee bar here sources their in-house brew from Cloud Picker, a local microroaster that prides themselves on using only quality green beans from traceable coffee farms. And a fine brew it is, too.

# MANNINGS BAKERY

*Old Dublin favorite*

**39-40 Thomas Street (near Meath Street)** / **+353 1 454 2114**
manningsbakeryshops.ie / Closed Sunday

Founded over 60 years ago, Mannings Bakery is something of an institution.
Well before the cupcake and artisan doughnut craze took the city by storm,
their humble coffee slice (jam and fresh cream sandwiched with squares of
light pastry and topped with glossy coffee-flavored icing) reigned supreme.
This treat, along with Manning's traditional Gur cake (dried fruits sandwiched
between two thin layers of pastry) and sugar-encrusted apple tart can still be
enjoyed at the café. Go on, indulge your sweet tooth and get a taste of Dublin
nostalgia while you're in the neighborhood.

# TEELING WHISKEY DISTILLERY

*Tours and tastings*

**13-17 Newmarket (near Mill Lane)**
**+353 1 531 0888 / teelingwhiskey.com**
**Open daily**

The Teeling family has been producing Irish whiskey since 1782, when Walter Teeling set up a small distillery in Marrowbone Lane. Back then, the city's whiskey industry was booming, with The Liberties even earning itself the nickname "Golden Triangle," in recognition of the number of distilleries in the area. Sadly, the business fell dormant in the 1970s, but two of the family's current generation — Jack and Stephen — have recently picked up the reins (hooray!), opening a new distillery and bringing the whiskey tradition back to the neighborhood. Just a short stroll from the original site, today's Teelings Distillery offers fully guided tours and whiskey tastings that run daily.

# THE GLAMOUR PIT

*Treat yourself*

**2 Meath Mart, Meath Street (near Meath Place)** / **+353 87 620 0724**
**facebook.com/theglamourpitdublin** / **Closed Sunday**

When Liberty belles need a pampering session they head straight for
The Glamour Pit. From up-dos and blow-drys to acrylics and smokey eyes,
this beauty salon offers the works. And all in lovely, friendly surroundings.
Above the whir of hairdryers, you'll hear constant laughter and banter
between the chatty staff and the locals, especially on the weekend, when
a party atmosphere takes over the salon. Keep an eye on their Facebook
page for updates on special offers – discounts usually pop up on Mondays
and Tuesdays.

# THE RIDDLER CAFÉ AND RESTAURANT

*Food with character*

**La Rochelle Building, High Street (near Lamb Alley)**
**+353 1 907 3266 / theriddler.ie / Open daily**

From buttermilk cakes to coffee named after weird and wonderful Dubliners, The Riddler Café and Restaurant draws on just about every local influence to deliver a unique Liberties dining experience. Grab a cup of "Johnny Forty Coats" coffee (named after an eccentric man who wandered around the city in the 1930s wearing what looked like 40 coats) or pull up a chair and ponder the many riddles emblazoned on the back wall as you wait to be served. Feeling adventurous? Try the hearty Riddler Stew. Chef Kym Gilbert puts her own spin on this classic Irish dish, partnering the hearty stew of braised beef, barley and root vegetables with her delicious homemade whiskey bread. It's a veritable hug in a bowl.

# but first, coffee

*Caffeinate in style*

### 3FE
32 Lower Grand Canal Street (at East Albert Place;
Georgian Dublin), +353 1 661 9329, 3fe.com
open daily

### BEANHIVE
26 Dawson Street (near St Stephen's Green; Grafton
Quarter), +353 1 677 4685, beanhive.ie, open daily

### COFFEE ANGEL
27 Lower Pembroke Street (at Pembroke Lane;
Georgian Dublin), +353 1 969 6002, coffeeangel.com
closed Sunday

### KAPH
31 Drury Street (near Castle Market; Creative
Quarter), +353 1 613 9030, kaph.ie, open daily

### LEGIT COFFEE CO
1 Meath Mart, Meath Street (near Engine Alley;
The Liberies), no phone, legitcoffeeco.com
closed Sunday

### NETWORK
39 Aungier Street (at Peter Row; Camden Quarter)
+353 87 953 5518, networkcafe.ie, open daily

### THE FUMBALLY
Fumbally Lane (near New Street South;
The Liberties), +353 1 529 8732
thefumbally.ie, closed Sunday and Monday

LEGIT
COFFEE CO.

THE
FUMBALLY

Independent cafés have taken Dublin by storm in recent years, transforming formerly derelict shops and businesses into hip hangouts and inviting work spaces. Wake up and smell the specialist coffee.

Run by Damien Vossion, **LEGIT Coffee Co.** serves up some of the best brews in The Liberties, including cups by the likes of Irish roaster Baobab. Drop in for the coffee, stay for homemade artisan sausage rolls and oven-fresh scones and pastries.

Back in 2008, Colin Harmon quit his office job to open his own café. Fast-forward to present day and not only is he the very proud owner of cool, minimalist **3FE** (short for Third Floor Espresso), he's also a champion barista. Plus, he's got his own roastery that sources single-origin beans from Bolivia and Guatemala.

With 3FE and Caravan Roastery on its menu combined with a reputation for producing highly photogenic, almost-too-beautiful-to-drink works of latte art, **Network**'s credentials are indeed excellent. As for counter treats, who could resist the crumbly oat cookies and gooey chocolate brownies?

At blink-and-you'd-miss-it café **Beanhive**, the playful baristas are renowned for their sense of fun, especially when it comes to latte art – who doesn't love a swirly rose or a smiley cartoon cat?

Passionate about brewing methods and fancy a tasting? **Coffee Angel** not only regularly churns out barista champions, but their coffee, sourced from Ethiopia, Kenya and Ecuador, has also made its way onto the menus of Michelin-starred restaurants around town.

Free WiFi: check. Comfy mismatched furniture: check. Liberal attitude toward dogs: check (they're even allowed inside!). Specialty coffee: CHECK. With a double shot of 3FE roast as standard, you might never want to leave **The Fumbally** – so stay.

When the weather gods shine on the Creative Quarter, the bench outside **Kaph** is the ultimate people-watching spot. The java is pretty amazing, too, whether you're after a flat white, matcha latte or soy-milk brew. There are eight types of grounds to choose from, all lightly roasted so that they release more caffeine and let you really taste the fruit. On a sunny day, make mine an iced coffee to-go.

# dublin 7

## hibsboro, smithfield, stoneybatter

Stoneybatter and its D7 hinterland is to Dublin as Shoreditch is to London and Williamsburg is to NYC. This young, vibrant hood is a hot spot for brunch joints, artisan stores and hip little places to caffeinate. Incorporating Smithfield, Phibsboro and Stoneybatter, this northern area of Dublin's inner city is teeming with culture, history and creativity. Discover an endearing "secret garden," watch ceramic artists at work and experience some of Ireland's most toe-tapping music sessions. A thriving foodie scene offers plenty of choice when it comes to eating out, whether you opt for pub grub or join a line for early morning eats.

1 Arran Street East (off map)
2 Cotto
3 Dice Bar
4 Dublin Vintage Factory
5 L. Mulligan Grocer
6 Light House Cinema
7 Lilliput Stores
8 Moo Market

# ARRAN STREET EAST

*Sustainable, hand-thrown ceramics*

**1 Little Green Street (at Mary's Lane) / +353 83 814 6672
arranstreeteast.ie / Closed Sunday**

Influenced by the earthy colors of the Victorian Fruit Market nearby, Arran Street East is a ceramics studio that specializes in producing sustainable handcrafted kitchenware and beautifully finished hand-thrown homeware. Their collection of tableware includes egg cups, mugs, plant pots, plates and soap dishes, and comes in a selection of natural hues named after produce, including cabbage, potato, parsnip, lemon, pomegranate and pink grapefruit. Fancy having a go yourself? The studio runs regular workshops in free-wheeling, throwing and glazing, as well as one-day courses in floristry. Visit their website for news on upcoming classes.

# COTTO

*Pizza and brunch joint*

46 Manor Street (near Aughrim Street) / +353 1 552 2918 / cotto.ie
Closed Monday and Tuesday

Situated on Manor Street, Cotto has built up a loyal following thanks to
its imaginative brunches, thin, tasty pizzas and generous salads. The décor
is simple, stripped-down and minimalist: think plywood, metal framed-
chairs, jam jars filled with tea lights, trailing houseplants and potted cacti.
Pizza-wise, I love the Ortolana, a veggie extravaganza of roasted zucchini,
eggplant, red pepper, artichoke and basil. For brunch, I recommend the
mushrooms on toast – wild mushrooms, Parmesan and a poached egg
on toasted brioche, fresh from the local Arun Bakery. And the coffee? It's
sourced from The Docklands' Cloud Picker roastery. Support local, indeed.

# DICE BAR

*NYC-style dive*

**79 Queen Street (at Benburb Street)** / **+353 1 633 3936**
**dicebar.com** / **Open daily**

Once owned by Huey Morgan of the band Fun Lovin' Criminals, Dice Bar has lovable New York attitude written all over it. Literally. Out front, an unmissable red neon sign exclaims "Phat Joint"; inside, however, the in-house craft brews – Revolution Red and Augustine Lager – are unmistakably Dublin. The watering hole also serves a good selection of other microbrews such as Sabotage IPA from Kildare and D'arcy's Dublin Stout, as well as Sparta from Bavaria and Bohemia. P.S. Their playlist of indie rock is so spot on that you may find yourself staying a little longer than expected just to listen to one more tune.

# DUBLIN VINTAGE FACTORY

*Fashion by the kilo*

**57 Smithfield Square (near Arran Quay)** / +353 1 872 7144
dublinvintagefactory.com / Open daily

Located rather fittingly in a 1950s garage, this secondhand clothing
and home goods warehouse sells pre-loved items by the kilo. The idea
is simple: you gather up as many bits and bobs from around the store
as you want, and then weigh them at the till when you're ready to
purchase. You're charged by weight, rather than per item, making it
a case of the more the merrier. With prices fixed at €20 (US$25) per
kilogram (heads up: 1kg is 2.2lbs), there are bargains galore, especially
if you're looking to pick up a good quality leather jacket, fur coat or
pair of old-school 501s at a knockdown price.

# L. MULLIGAN GROCER

*Craft whiskies, beers and pub grub*

**18 Stoneybatter (at Arbour Place) / +353 1 670 9889**
**lmulligangrocer.com / Open daily**

Much like Mary's Bar and Hardware (see pg 100), the owners of here have kitted out the pub with the past firmly in mind. Glass jars filled with candy keep watch over the bar, while the menu (heavy on whiskey) is presented within an old, hardcover book – definitely a novel way to decide on your drink. If you're jonesing for something to nibble, the food menu is of the gastropub variety (there's free-range chicken Kiev, vegetarian haggis and three different types of Scotch eggs), and includes beer pairings. As for the grocery aspect, they stock each and every craft beer brewed in Ireland, so if your taste buds are curious to go beyond whiskey, you'll be in for an adventure. Just don't ask for Guinness: this is one of the only bars in Dublin that doesn't serve that specific stout.

# LIGHT HOUSE CINEMA

*Boutique movie theater*

**Market Square, Smithfield (near Queen Street)** / **+353 1 872 8006**
**lighthousecinema.ie** / **Open daily**

The four-screen, 600-seat Light House Cinema at Smithfield offers one of Dublin's most unique cinema experiences. Not only does it screen a mix of local, independent, foreign-language, arthouse and classic movies, but there's also an on-site bar where you can enjoy an adult beverage, before, after or even during your movie – if you're willing to get up to order. The snack choice at the cinema's café is a cut above, too, with freshly made soups, superfood salads, gourmet sausage rolls – black pudding and pear, and fennel and chili to name but two – and freshly baked cakes and pastries. A win-win-win, for sure.

# LILLIPUT STORES

*Friendly grocer*

**5 Rosemount Terrace, Arbour Hill (at Viking Place) / +353 1 672 9516**
**lilliputstores.com / Open daily**

This neighborhood supermarket is a greengrocer, deli and coffee shop all rolled into one, and has been part and parcel of Stoneybatter street life since 2007. Lilliput Stores source as much of their produce as possible locally, which means you'll find Irish and international cheese, charcuterie, freshly baked breads and pastries, as well as fresh seasonal fruit and vegetables. For lunch on the run, there's sandwiches, soups and stews prepared daily. Coffee is top-notch too, roasted weekly by County Meath-based Ariosa Coffee Roasting Company.

# MOO MARKET

*Café and gift shop*

**29 Stoneybatter (near Arbour Place)** / **+353 1 537 1476**
**facebook.com/MooMarket.ie** / **Closed Sundays**

One part cute gift and interiors shop, one part cake-laden café, Moo Market is one of the prettiest shops in Stoneybatter. Run by former school teacher Aisling Moran, who is all about sourcing local products, the boutique stocks sweet little Gaelic-language greeting cards by Cartai Rubai, hand-knitted soft toys, locally produced prints, handmade soaps and colorful handcrafted jewelry. The coffee is superb and comes from Dublin-based roastery Upside. Grab your bag of purchased goodies, a slice of rocky road and a flat white, and enjoy on the terrace out front.

# café society

*Sip and socialize*

## A SLICE OF CAKE CAFÉ
56 Manor Place (near Norseman Place;
Stoneybatter), +353 1 445 6100
asliceofcake.ie, open daily

## BIBI'S
14B Emorville Avenue (near Ovoca Road; Portobello)
+353 1 454 742, bibis.ie, open daily

## CAFE NOTTO
79 Thomas Street (near Thomas Street;
The Liberties), +353 1 454 7223, no website
open daily

## EMER'S KITCHEN
102 Leeson Street (near Leeson Lane; Georgian
Dublin), +353 1 89 251 2038, facebook.com/
EmersKitchen, closed Saturday and Sunday

## MEET ME IN THE MORNING
50 Pleasants Street (near Pleasants Lane;
Portobello), no phone, facebook.com/
meetmeinthemorningcafe, closed Monday

## TWO BOYS BREW
75 North Circular Road (near Royal Canal Bank;
Phibsboroughugh), no phone, twoboysbrew.ie
open daily

TWO BOYS BREW

When it comes to top-notch coffee, great brekkies, healthy lunches and lazy brunches, Dubliners have never had it so good.

If it's breakfast, get thee to **Meet Me in the Morning.** This mellow eatery with a dreamy name (borrowed from a Bob Dylan song) is all the motivation you need to rise and shine. As soon as you walk through the door, you're greeted by the menu, handwritten on a mirror like a cheeky love note. Wake up your taste buds with Turkish eggs, spiced hash potatoes, crunchy granola and, my personal go-to, sourdough toast topped with homemade hazelnut and cacao butter paired with excellent specialty coffee from Danish roaster La Cabra.

Simplicity is key at **Bibi's** is a lovely, homey café headed up by a brother-sister team. There's just the right amount of choice no matter what time you drop in – no FOMO, no drawn-out deliberations. If it's lunchtime, be sure to grab a chorizo, Manchego and sundried-tomato pan-fried sandwich. Melty perfection.

Loitering is something very much frowned upon at **Emer's Kitchen**, which is probably for the best. Given the option, you'd likely never want to leave their nommy cakes, salads and delicious cups of joe made with beans from County Cork's Badger & Dodo. But with St Stephen's Green Park (see pg 126) on their doorstep, who needs tables and chairs anyway?

Over in Stoneybatter, it's more of a sit-down affair at **A Slice of Cake Café**. In fact, their boozy, all-day weekend brunches are best enjoyed whilst lounging. But tasty, everyday goodies like French toast and 3FE (see pg 20) coffee mean you don't have to wait until Saturday and Sunday to treat yourself either.

The lads at **Two Boys Brew** are no strangers to a bit of sweet temptation, and their café has got plenty of savory delights, too. For every sinful chocolate cookie, there's a virtuous superfood salad or a homemade Bircher bowl, as well as my brunch-time choice, the chili- and lime-infused avocado on sourdough.

For friendly neighborhood eats in The Liberties look no further than **Cafe Notto**. This airy, light-filled noshery is a great place to get some work done if you've brought your laptop. If not, grab a coffee and a slice of carrot cake and watch the world go by from one of the big windows that looks out onto Thomas Street.

# the quays

Immortalized in art in Jack B. Yeats' 1923 painting *The Liffey Swim*, and in literature courtesy of James Joyce's *The Dead*, the North and South Quays have long captured the imagination of local creatives. Running either side of the River Liffey, The Quays are connected by a series of bridges, the most iconic of which is the pedestrianized Ha'penny Bridge. Take a walk on the wild side and check out the hip barbershops, tattoo studios and music bars of the South Quays, before wandering across the Liffey to slightly more sedate surroundings. Be sure to arrive hungry though – from sublime Dublin grub to low-cal salads to gluttonous desserts, an epicurean odyssey awaits on the North Quays.

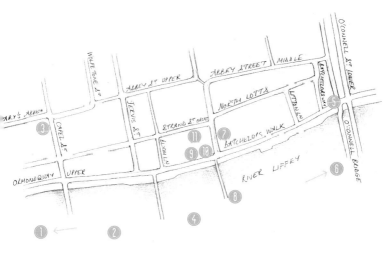

1  Bagots Hutton (off map)
2  Bison Bar
3  Brother Hubbard North
4  Cut & Sew (off map)
5  PÓG
6  Theatre Upstairs (off map)

7  The Bakehouse
8  The Clockwork Door
9  The Winding Stair
10 The Wooden Mills
11 Yamamori Sushi

# BAGOTS HUTTON

*Drinks, eats and tunes*

**6 Upper Ormond Quay (near Capel Street)** / **+353 1 878 8118**
**bagotshutton.com** / **Open daily**

Having built up a loyal following at their cozy premises on South William
Street, Giovanni Viscardi and Brian Deery of Bagots Hutton recently decided
to spread their wings and export their brand of New York basement charm
across the Liffey to Ormond Quay. Inside the concept space, the décor is a
punchy palette of yellow and gray, with three unique areas (café, wine bar,
basement-level restaurant and a stage for live entertainment). Regular jazz
performances accompany the menu of pizza, steak and light Mediterranean
bites – check their social media channels for upcoming events. Fancy a tasty
memento? Vino, teas and cheeses are just some of the items on sale in the
store within the cafe.

# BISON BAR

*Saddle up for whiskies and BBQ feasts*

**11 Wellington Quay (near Sycamore Street) / +353 86 056 3144**
**bisonbar.ie / Open daily**

From the wagon-wheel nailed to the wall above the door to the spaghetti-western style signage, one look at Bison Bar and you know you're in for some serious fun. Pony up to the bar and take your pick from over 150 different types of whiskey before tucking in to a smoky barbecue feast of pulled pork, spare ribs and spicy chicken wings that are completely worth the mess. All meats are slow roasted for 14 hours in an American Southern Pride Smoker to guarantee melt-in-the-mouth perfection. Yee-haw.

# BROTHER HUBBARD NORTH

*Tastes of the Middle East*

**153 Capel Street
(at Upper Abbey Street)
+353 1 441 1112
brotherhubbard.ie / Open daily**

Don't be fooled by the clean lines and utilitarian styling of Brother Hubbard – this café is as famous for the hospitality of owners Garrett Fitzgerald and James Boland as it is for its delicious Middle Eastern-inspired menu. For brunch, I love their Turkish eggs menemen (spicy scrambled eggs with tomato and paprika-roasted peppers, feta and olive yogurt, sourdough and salsa). The coffee served is all single-origin brew from 3FE (see pg 20), while their tea comes from Wall & Keogh (see pg 76). For a sugary hit, try their deliciously rich, ganache-based hot chocolate or savor a sticky helping of freshly baked baklava.

# CUT & SEW

*A cut above*

**31 Wellington Quay (near Eustace Street) / +353 83 472 4447**
**cutandsew.ie / Closed Sunday**

Sean Bryan started Cut & Sew as a pop-up barbershop in the basement of a Temple Bar record store before moving to this brick-and-mortar fit-out. Clean cuts such as the classic bald fade, styled with their own brand of sea salt spray, and the modish side part pompadour created using a clipper-over-comb technique brought gents in, but the thumping tunes and urban vibe cemented the cult following. The barbers now hold in-salon training and courses for those interested in the trade. As for the "sew" aspect of the name, look out for the shop's apparel and accessories in the salon.

# PÓG

*Healthy options made with love*

**32 Bachelors Walk (at Bachelors Way) / +353 1 878 3255**
**ifancyapog.ie / Open daily**

Pronounced "pogue" (the Irish Gaelic word for "kiss"), Póg specializes in freshly prepared salads, juices, healthy breakfasts and frozen yogurt. Either pull up a seat inside their pretty, candy-colored café or order to go — all dishes come complete with calorie and protein information, taking all the guess work out of dining out. For a guilt-free treat, I recommend their protein pancakes. Served with granola, strawberries and banana, they're naturally sweet and make for the perfect post-gym reward.

# THEATRE UPSTAIRS

*Pub with a stage*

**10-11 Eden Quay (near Marlborough Street)** / **+353 85 772 7375**
**theatreupstairs.ie** / **Closed Sunday and Monday**

Nestled above Lanigan's Bar, Theatre Upstairs is an independently run,
44-seat playhouse that showcases new works by Irish writers. It's Ireland's
only theatre dedicated to staging the world premieres of new plays, and
they recently partnered with the Edinburgh Festival Fringe to host preview
shows for a number of the comedians. A light lunch is included in the ticket
price at matinees (usually freshly made soup of the day and homemade
brown bread), and special dinner-and-a-show deals are available for evening
performances. In addition to producing and staging plays, Theatre Upstairs
also runs a readers group to help new playwrights with script development
for new productions. All in all, a very worthwhile experience.

# THE BAKEHOUSE

*Freshly baked cakes and breads*

**6 Bachelors Walk (at Lower Liffey Street)** / **+353 1 873 4279**
**the-bakehouse.ie** / **Open daily**

With its eye-popping palette of pink, black and white, this café is hard to miss. Inside, the menu focuses on tasty sweet and savory eats that generations of Dubliners were raised on – from Dublin Coddle (a salty stew of potatoes, sausages and bacon) to luscious coffee slices and squares of Gur cake (an old staple akin to a fruit cake). I love their brunch menu – especially the choice of breads that accompany most dishes. For a taste of traditional Dublin, go for a toasted slice of turnover, batch or brown soda bread, and enjoy with lashings of Irish butter.

# THE CLOCKWORK DOOR

*Pay-as-you-stay home away from home*

**51 Wellington Quay (at Asdill's Row)** / **+353 1 538 0998**
**clockworkdoor.ie** / **Open daily**

The Clockwork Door is Ireland's first "time house," a pay-by-the-minute space where you can drink as much tea and coffee as you like, eat biscuits and partake of the Wi-Fi, and only pay for the time you spend there. After seeing similar ventures in Russia and Germany, founder Ciaran Hogan decided to bring the idea to his hometown. The comfortable, alcohol-free venue is split into six homey rooms where you're welcome to listen to music, play board games or video games, read or watch movies. The venue also hosts regular evening events including open-mic slam poetry, quiz nights and interactive cinema screenings where the audience decides how the plot takes shape by voting for scene options via a smartphone app. Drop on by, even if only for a quick snack and cuppa.

# THE WINDING STAIR

*Bookshop and Irish cuisine*

**40 Lower Ormond Quay (near Lower Liffey Street) / + 353 1 872 7320
winding-stair.com / Open daily**

Borrowing its name from a collection of poems by William Butler Yeats – as well
as the higgledy-piggledy staircase inside – this restaurant-slash-bookshop's
location is as picture-perfect as it gets. Downstairs, the wonderfully quaint
bookstore is well-stocked with all sorts of titles, from local interest to kid lit,
cookery books to poetry. Plus, wine is also available. After you've leafed through
some tomes and finished your vino, move upstairs to the restaurant. It not only
serves up some of the best cuisine in the city (the creamy seafood chowder is
incredible), but also stunning views of the Ha'penny Bridge and River Liffey.
No prizes for guessing why this little gem has been a favorite meeting place
for writers, musicians and artists since the 1970s.

# THE WOOLLEN MILLS

*Casual bites and Liffey views*

**42 Lower Ormond Quay (at Lower Liffey Street)** / **+353 1 828 0835**
**thewoollenmills.com** / **Open daily**

Formerly a haberdashery and drapery shop (that once employed James Joyce no less), The Woollen Mills is now an ever-reliable spot for brunch and low-key eats. Inside, it's all about industrial-chic, with white-washed walls, exposed piping and subway tiles. But up on the roof terrace, it's a whole other story. Lightbulbs and fairy lights create a cozy vibe, outshone only by the lovely birds-eye view of the river. As for what to order, the butternut squash bhaji served with baby spinach, poached egg, tangy mango marmalade and a dollop of sheep's yogurt makes for a spicy little alternative to the full Irish "Ha'penny fry up".

# YAMAMORI SUSHI

*Sashimi, rolls and weekend Tengu bar*

**38/39 Lower Ormond Quay (near Lower Liffey Street)**
**+353 1 872 0003 / yamamori.ie / Open daily**

For light raw fish bites and Asian-influenced dishes you can't go wrong with Yamamori. It's located on bustling Ormond Quay, but as soon as you step inside this restaurant, a calm ambiance takes over. My favorite offering is the crayfish- and cucumber-filled Norimaki rainbow roll, which is perfect for sharing, and makes this spot a great choice if you're dining out with a group. On the weekend, don't miss the Tengu set-up out back where whiskey, cocktails and tunes flow until the early hours of the morning.

# culture vulture

*Offbeat museums and galleries*

### EPIC THE IRISH EMIGRATION MUSEUM
CHQ, Custom House Quay (near Exchange Place;
Docklands), +353 1 906 0861, epicchq.com, open daily

### GALLERY OF PHOTOGRAPHY
Meeting House Square (near Sycamore Street;
Temple Bar), + 353 1 671 4654
galleryofphotography.ie, open daily

### JAM ART FACTORY
64/65 Patrick Street (near South Dillon Place;
The Liberties), +353 1 616 5671, jamartfactory.com
open daily

### NCAD GALLERY
100 Thomas Street (near Meath Street;
The Liberties), +353 1 636 4390
ncad.ie/about/gallery, closed Saturday and Sunday

### THE ICON FACTORY
3 Aston Place (near Bedford Lane; South Quays),
+353 86 202 4533, iconfactorydublin.ieopen daily

### THE LITTLE MUSEUM OF DUBLIN
15 St Stephen's Green (at Dawson Street;
Grafton Quarter), +353 1 661 1000, littlemuseum.ie
open daily

Looking to make the most of a rainy afternoon in Dublin? I know just the place.

An offshoot of the National College of Art and Design, **NCAD Gallery** stages regular multimedia exhibitions by students and up-and-coming international artists from its Harry Clarke House building. FYI: former college alumni include designers Orla Kiely and Philip Treacy, as well as WB Yeats. If that's not reason enough to check out the local talent, I don't know what is.

Housed in a glorious Georgian building, T**he Little Museum of Dublin** sets out to tell the story of 20th century Dublin in just half an hour. One of the things I love most about this museum is the randomness of the artifacts on display. From newspaper cuttings about early U2 gigs to the lectern used by JFK during his visit, to leftovers from the booming Celtic Tiger years (who's for some gold leaf Monster Munch?), there's plenty of food for thought.

Delving further into the Irish psyche, Temple Bar's **Gallery of Photography** is home to around 5 million images that provide a wonderful glimpse into social change in Dublin and Ireland. Entry is free, plus they regularly run photography courses as well as exhibitions by well-known international photographers.

Fact: a whopping 70 million people worldwide claim to have Irish ancestry. Through a series of interactive exhibits, **EPIC The Irish Emigration Museum** uncovers the stories of Irish emigrants and the ways they and their descendants (hello, Barack Obama) have contributed to the modern world. You might even learn a thing or two about your own family tree at the museum's Irish Family History Centre.

Speaking of Irish roots, **The Icon Factory** gallery is chock-full of local legends. It's a non-profit run by the artists behind the eye-popping Icon Walk, which features depictions of the Irish poets, writers and rock stars that have redefined the once grimy backstreets of Temple Bar. If you like what you see out there, pop inside to check out the rest.

Located in the heart of The Liberties, **Jam Art Factory** is an independent gallery and design shop managed by brothers John and Mark Haybryne that showcases top Irish design. The creations of 50 local artists are shown here, and their work includes ceramics and textiles, jewelry, street art, illustrations and prints that all have one thing in common – an irresistibly cheeky edge.

# temple bar

---

Postcard-worthy cobbles, pricey pints and live music bars make Temple Bar the tourist epicenter of Dublin. Scratch the surface, though, and for every full-to-bursting pub you encounter, you'll find a little gem of a clothing store, café or restaurant waiting to be discovered. There's culture, too – plenty of it, from photography exhibits to gallery shows by up-and-coming artists to open-air performances by street artists and buskers. From May to September, the Wednesday night arts and crafts markets bring a touch of homespun magic, while year-round, the Icon Walk celebrates the crème de la crème of street art. Last but not least, don't miss the colorful murals featuring the likenesses of Seamus Heaney, Shane McGowan, James Joyce and Phil Lynott. Instagram at the ready.

1 April and the Bear
2 DiFontaine's Pizza
3 Find
4 Folkster
5 Indigo & Cloth
6 Roberta's
7 Rosa Madre
8 Siopaella
9 The Gutter Bookshop

# APRIL AND THE BEAR

*Gorgeous home goods*

**1 Cows Lane (near West Essex Street) / +353 1 616 9888**
**aprilandthebear.com / Closed Tuesday**

April and the Bear, a former pop-up store, recently put down permanent roots, and hallelujah for that. It's a little wonderland of lighting, gifts and art that's all carefully selected by owner Siobhan Lam. I love the cute, local wit captured in their wall prints – particularly the one that proclaims, "Indecision is my superpower" as well as the debonair-looking giraffe swathed in a plaid scarf– and adore their notebooks and stationery. I've definitely got my eye on their amazing wallpaper selection, which includes prints of tropical palm leaves, pineapples and a Chinese floral pattern. Actually, if I'm being honest, there's nothing in this shop I wouldn't take home with me.

# DIFONTAINE'S PIZZA

*Late-night eats*

22 Parliament Street (near Wellington Quay) / +353 1 674 5485
difontainespizzeria.ie / Open daily

When it's 3am and only pizza will do, DiFontaine's is the place to grab a hot slice or calzone. Inside, there's a small seating area, and the NYC influence is obvious from the red-and-white subway tile to the photos of Manhattan that adorn the walls to the pies named after streets and landmarks, like The Delancey and The Radio City. The owners lived in New York for many years and even flew the oven in from the Big Apple. I usually go for The Limelight, made with broccoli, tomato and mushroom. In a giving mood? Opt into their pay-it-forward initiative. When you order for yourself, but pay a little extra, they put the food you paid for on hold and then give it to someone in need – usually a well-deserving local charity partner.

54

# FIND

*Something old, something new*

**Cows Lane (near Copper Alley)**
**+353 1 679 9790** / findonline.ie
 Open daily

There's a lovely granny's attic charm to this gift and houseware shop. Crammed with up-cycled furniture, vintage maps, 1930's mirrors, DIY chalk paint, small religious statuettes of St. Jude, Jesus and the Virgin Mary, and limited edition prints by local artists such as Salty Philip, you never quite know what you'll come across inside. Tempting as it is to lug home one of their antique birdcages, their selection of locally crafted Candella soya wax candles and organic lotions and skincare potions by Dublin Herbalists make for sweet-smelling (and way more practical) souvenirs.

# FOLKSTER

*Folkin' lovely*

**9 Eustace Street (near Meeting House Square) / + 353 1 675 0917
folkster.com / Open daily**

Founded by Irish stylist Blanaid Hennessy, Folkster is one part dress-up box, one part gorgeous interior design store. I love this shop for its eclectic mix of formal wear and cool accessories. Inside there's footwear, bags and casual pieces galore, but turn left and you enter a walk-in wardrobe with rail upon rail of beaded gowns, cocktail dresses and one-off showstoppers. Gift shopping? Head to the back and browse the souk-style stalls laden with glassware, ceramics and other fancy trinkets.

# INDIGO & CLOTH

*Specialist coffee and cool threads*

**9 Essex Street (near Sycamore Street)** / **+353 1 670 6403**
**indigoandcloth.com** / **Open daily**

Gareth Pitcher is one of Dublin's hardest working entrepreneurs. He owns and manages a men's clothing store, a creative studio and a brew bar in partnership with the guys from Clement & Pekoe (See pg 76) — all from the same four-story building on Essex Street. Welcome to Indigo & Cloth. Pop in for a coffee, some tunes and check out the interesting collection of menswear labels including Sandqvist bags from Sweden, clothing from Denmark's Norse Projects and footwear by British designer Oliver Spencer. Many of these can't be found anywhere else in the city, making your sartorial purchases all the more sweet.

# ROBERTA'S

*Restaurant, cocktail bar and weekend brunch spot*

**1 East Essex Street (at Crane Lane) / +353 1 616 9612 / robertas.ie
Open daily**

First things first, prepare to be blown away by the gorgeous surrounds here. From the glass atrium and tropical-looking roof terrace to the zebra stripes beneath your feet, a visit to Roberta's is as much about drinking in the surroundings as it is about quaffing cocktails or indulging in their mouthwatering menu of wood-fired pizzas and steak. Here for brunch? Their eggs Benedict is definitely the way to go, and it's always worth asking about the weekend juice offerings, too; you can count on the zingy beetroot and ginger to piece you back together if last night's excesses have left you feeling in any way fragile.

# ROSA MADRE

*Real deal Italian*

**7 Crow Street (near Cecilia Street) / +353 1 551 1206**
**rosamadre.ie / Open daily**

Forget plastic-coated menus filled with photos of mediocre-looking spaghetti and lasagna; when it comes to authentic Italian eats in this hood, Rosa Madre is the only place to go. Luca, the owner, makes sure of it. Seafood is a specialty here and it's always fresh and local. I adore the paccheri al frutti di mare, made with large, tubular noodles, prawns, squid, clams and mussels in a fresh, tangy tomato sauce, but if you're looking for a daily special, just ask Luca, he'll be more than happy to passionately tell you about what goes into each dish and where the ingredients came from. Fair warning: reservations are advised as this is a busy spot, especially at weekends.

# SIOPAELLA

*Pre-loved designer finds*

**25A South Temple Lane (at Cecilia Street)** / **+353 1 677 9106**
**siopaella.com** / **Open daily**

Pronounced "shuppa-ella," this designer swap shop takes its name from the Irish-Gaelic word for shop, "siopa" and the owner's first name, Ella. Founded by Canadian (and honorary Dubliner) Ella de Guzman, Siopaella lets you buy, sell, exchange or part-exchange (aka, trade for store credit) name brand handbags, jewelry and clothing mint-condition. Keep an eye on the shop's Instagram feed for new arrivals. Siopaella 's team of stylists regularly post suspense-filled unboxing videos, showcasing beautiful, still-in-original-packaging designer pieces. Sigh. A girl can dream.

# THE GUTTER BOOKSHOP

*Literary goldmine*

**Cow's Lane (at West Essex Street)    +353 1 679 9206**
**gutterbookshop.com    Open daily**

The gutter refernced at The Gutter Bookshop is taken from Oscar Wilde's quip
"We are all in the gutter, but some of us are looking at the stars". Inspired by
this quote, owner Bob Johnston has set out to create a unique and uplifting
bookish space. Torn between two covers? My recommendation is to head
straight for the staff picks section, as their selections have never let me
down. Anyone shopping for younger readers will find the children's section
is especially well-stocked.

# to market

*Baubles, bites and books*

### COW'S LANE DESIGNER MART
Cow's Lane (at Copper Alley; Temple Bar)
+353 87 655 5806, facebook.com/DesignerMart
open Saturday, June through September

### EATYARD
9-10 South Richmond Street (near Harcourt Road;
Portobello), no phone, the-eatyard.com
open Thursday through Sunday

### GEORGE'S STREET ARCADE
South Great George's Street (near Fade
Street; Creative Quarter), +353 283 6077
georgesstreetarcade.com, open daily

### TEMPLE BAR BOOK MARKET
Temple Bar Square (near Crane Lane; Temple Bar),
+353 86 190 2892, facebook.com/The-Temple-Bar-
Book-Market-Page, open Saturday and Sunday

### TEMPLE BAR FOOD MARKET
Meeting House Square (near Eustace Street;
Temple Bar), +353 1 905 9189, facebook.com/
TempleBarFoodMarket, open Saturday

### THE HA'PENNY FLEA MARKET
The Grand Social, 35 Lower Liffey Street (near
Strand Street Great; North Quay), +353 1 874 0076
thegrandsocial.ie/market, open Saturday

EATYARD

For unique finds and tasty organic eats, not to mention colorful street-life, look no further than Dublin's markets.

Every weekend at **Temple Bar Book Market** you can browse the random haul of new, secondhand and antique books, as well as vinyl records. There's everything and anything from Pearl Jam and Metallica albums to Elvis fanzines, Irish-language poetry books and faded, leather-bound French novels.

Just a short stroll away, the Saturday stalls at **Temple Bar Food Market** are waiting to seduce you with sizzling burgers, mouth-watering burritos, healthy juices, locally made cheese, jams and preserves, drool-worthy treats from producers such as Kilbeggan Handmade Chocolate.

Crossing the Liffey, The Grand Social's indoor **Ha'penny Flea Market** hosts a marvelous mix of goods from vintage clothing to designer wares, vinyl, retro furniture, jewelry and books, accompanied by live music. This is a great place to pick up a unique piece from emerging artisans.

Speaking of up-and-comers, every Saturday **Cow's Lane Designer Mart** showcases some of Dublin's finest creative talent. Held outdoors from June to September, market stalls teem with handcrafted ceramics and wood-turned objects, as well as clothing, accessories and wall art. Don't miss Eimear Brennan's whimsical pen and ink prints of forest creatures – all include a secret short story or literary quote on the back.

Over in the Creative Quarter, **George's Street Arcade**'s beautiful red-brick Victorian building is home to the city's oldest enclosed market. First opened in 1881, the arcade holds an eclectic array of venues and eateries. Open daily, there's plenty to browse, from pre-loved clothing and paintings to vinyl records and handcrafted baubles.

Meanwhile, next to The Bernard Shaw (see pg 88), there's street food galore at **Eatyard**, the food market that rolls in every Thursday through Sunday. From the exotic delights of Kerala Kitchen (the chana saag with cumin and fennel is top notch), to Pitt Bros' barbecued feasts and authentic Sicilian eats from Pasta Box (the arancini are amazing), this little patch of Portobello is a foodie's dream. The local street art is pretty outstanding, too.

# the creative quarter

Oscar Wilde once said, "I can resist anything except temptation." We can but speculate on the heady enticements to which he alluded, but if the chink in your own armor is a less-hedonistic spot of retail indulgence, then temptation awaits in every nook of this area. From the market stalls of the historic George's Street Arcade (see pg 62), to the fashion and vintage shops of the Powerscourt Centre, not to mention the wonderful Irish design stores, trinkets and treats will lure you in at every turn. As you wander South William Street, George's Street, Drury Street and Exchequer Street, you'll be hard pushed to resist the charms of this gorgeous neighborhood. It's one of the best places to shop and spend an afternoon in Dublin: independent boutiques mingle with artists' studios, hair salons, jewelry designers and diverse food joints. What's more, whimsical red-brick Victorian buildings, candy-striped awnings and sweet little shopfronts make this is one of the most photogenic corners of the city. Ready for your close-up?

1  Appassionata Flowers
2  Article
3  Cocoa Atelier
4  Designist
5  Fallon & Byrne
6  Industry & Co.
7  Om Diva
8  San Lorenzo's
9  Skinfull Affairs
10 Ukiyo

# APPASSIONATA FLOWERS

*Lovely blossoms*

**29 Drury Street (at Castle Market)** / +353 1 672 9425
**appassionata.ie** / Closed Sunday

Drury Street is teeming with good looking shops and cafés, but this florist may just be the fairest of them all. With a background in TV production, managing director Ruth Monahan is no stranger to creating show-stopping spectacles. On first impressions, the shopfront has a *Secret Garden* quality to it that makes it impossible not to wonder what's inside. From lavish bouquets of roses to cute glass jars filled with wild berries and blooms, Appassionata offers countless ways to say it with flowers. And if you can't find what you're looking for here, their studio on South Cumberland Street will be only too happy to oblige.

# ARTICLE

*All the pretty things*

**Powerscourt Townhouse, South William Street (near Coppinger Row)**
**+353 1 679 9268 / articledublin.com / Open daily**

The jewel of the Creative Quarter, South William Street's Powerscourt Townhouse was once owned by Richard Wingfield, Third Viscount Powerscourt and his wife, Lady Amelia, who were renowned for throwing wild and decadent parties here. Today, this beautiful building plays host to a unique shopping experience, with over 40 specialist boutiques and restaurants under its roof. In Lord Powerscourt's former dressing room, you'll find Article, a carefully curated collection of homeware, trinkets and furniture. Tip: The quirky, Irish-designed notebooks and stationery make for excellent gifts and souvenirs.

# COCOA ATELIER

*French fancies*

**30 Drury Street (near Castle Market)** / **+353 1 675 3616**
**facebook.com/cocoaatelier** / **Open daily**

This cute-as-a-button chocolate boutique was founded in 2009 by
French chef Marc Amand and his Irish wife Mary Massy. From chocolates
and truffles to pastel colored macarons and sticky éclairs, every treat is
handmade with the purest of ingredients, including cocoa beans sourced
from Chocolaterie de l'Opéra in France. The hot chocolate here is one of
the best I've ever tried: made from a ganache base,it's rich, filling and
tastes like you're drinking melted chocolate neat. Nom.

# DESIGNIST

*Irresistible Irish designs*

**68 South Great George's Street (at St George's Mall)**
**+353 1 475 8534 / shop.designist.ie / Open daily**

Anne Lynott, Jennie Flynn and Barbara Nolan are the brains behind this gorgeous design and home goods store. They've been collaborating with Irish and international designers since 2010 to offer beautiful, well-made products at affordable price points. With everything in the shop retailing for under €100 (US$106), it's easy to get carried away, especially when shopping for gifts. Traveling light? You can't go wrong with a Dublin-themed print by a local illustrator. I have a turquoise illustrated map of Dublin at home and I love it. I also adore their cheeky Irish-designed greetings cards. P.S. Anyone looking to learn more about the city and its architecture will thoroughly enjoy their range of coffee table books.

# FALLON & BYRNE

*A foodie's paradise*

**11–17 Exchequer Street (near Dame Court)** / **+353 1 472 1010**
**fallonandbyrne.com** / **Open daily**

As luck would have it, Fallon & Byrne opened its doors just in time to coincide with my first job on nearby St Andrew's Street. You could say it was love at first bite. Located in a former telephone exchange building, on the ground floor there's a vibrant food hall with deli counters, artisan coffee and shelves heaving with culinary goodies and organic produce. Upstairs, an elegant restaurant serves seasonal dishes as well as vegan-friendly eats, while in the basement, the wine cellar stocks over 600 bottles, with many available to try by the glass.

# INDUSTRY & CO.

*Healthy bites and beautiful homeware*

**41A/B Drury Street (near Exchequer Street)** / **+353 1 613 9111**
**industryandco.com** / **Open daily**

Brother and sister team Vanessa and Marcus Mac Innes have curated a stylish
mix of old, new, industrial and recycled furniture, lighting and accessories
at their lifesty le boutique.  All items are handpicked based on their beauty,
quality, functionality and originality: look out for ceramics by Dublin 7's
Arran Street East (see pg 24) and jewelry from Irish label Isle. They're just as
selective about what goes into their café. Expect a delicious assortment of
freshly baked cakes, artisan coffee and healthy homemade soups and salads,
all made in-house. Gotta run? No worries. All dishes are available for takeout,
in biodegradable containers, no less. They've thought of everything.

# OM DIVA
*Fashion HQ*

**27 Drury Street (near Castle Market)** / **+353 1 679 1211**
**omdivaboutique.com** / **Open daily**

Is it a concept store? Is it a vintage shop? Is it an artist's studio? Well, it's all three actually. Founded by Ruth Ní Loinsigh in 2005, Om Diva started out as a market stall inspired by Ruth's backpacking adventures in India. Now spread over three floors, the multi-concept shop incorporates a contemporary section on the ground floor featuring clothing and accessories; the label upstairs, Atelier 27, showcases jewelry and womenswear by local designers, and the Aladdin's cave of a basement is filled with unique vintage finds from all over the world.

# SAN LORENZO'S

*Where Brooklyn meets Dublin*

**9 Castle House, 73-83 South Great George's Street (near Exchequer Street) / +353 1 478 9383 / sanlorenzos.ie / Open daily**

With its New York-sized portions, bold flavors and casual interior, locals flock to San Lorenzo's for brunch, lunch and dinner. I've had my fair share of all three here and can thoroughly recommend this spot, especially if you're celebrating a special occasion. The menu is Italian with a New York accent, but all ingredients are seasonal and locally sourced in Ireland. On weekends don't miss San Lorenzo's legendary brunch of champions – the menu includes 8 oz. steaks, crab cakes, eggs royale with caviar, a smashing list of aperitifs and luscious desserts, like the buttermilk salted caramel panna cotta – a guaranteed cure for the morning after the night before.

# SKINFULL AFFAIRS

*Guilt-free glamour*

**34 Exchequer Street (near South Williams Street)** / **+353 1 616 9933**
**facebook.com/skinfullaffairs** / **Open daily**

This beauty and nail bar is one of the first in Dublin to offer a complete range of natural and organic beauty products and skin treatments including massage, facials and microdermabrasion. Inside, it has a refreshing, almost rainforest feel to it, with lush green plants covering the walls and simple wooden shelves stocked with bottles and jars. My product pick is the vegan, chemical-free Ella + Mila nail polish. Whenever I pop in for a file and polish, my go-to is the strawberry milkshake-colored "Dessert Island".

# UKIYO

*Sing for your supper*

**9 Exchequer Street (at Dame Court)** / **+353 1 633 4071**
**ukiyobar.com** / **Open daily**

Ukiyo sits unassuming on a corner, but I'll let you in on a secret: this restaurant and bar has been serving up good times and great cocktails since 2004. The Japanese/Korean menu offers something for everyone, from sushi to beef bulgogi to tofu steak. By far the best thing about Ukiyo though is its basement karaoke where you'll find three private booths that each hold between 10 to 20 people. If you're a scaredy cat when it comes to singing in public, the privacy of the three booths, which can be booked by the hour if you've had dinner there, makes it much easier to belt out a bit of Beyoncé or whatever else takes your fancy.

# tea time

*Pinkies up!*

### CLEMENT & PEKOE
50 South William Street (near chatham Row; Creative Quarter), no phone, clementandpekoe.com, open daily

### OOLONG FLOWER POWER
4 Lower Stephens Street (near Dawson Street; Camden Quarter), +353 1 475 8422, oolongflowerpower.ie, open daily

### QUEEN OF TARTS
4 Cork Hill (at Dame Street; Temple Bar)
+353 1 633 4681, queenoftarts.ie, open daily

### TEA GARDEN
7 Lower Ormond Quay (near Capel Street; North Quay)
+353 86 219 1010, tea-garden.eu, open daily

### THE MERRION HOTEL
Upper Merrion Street (near Fitzwilliam Lane; Georgian Dublin), +353 1 603 0600, merrionhotel.com/drawingrooms_tea.php, open daily

### THE PEPPER POT
Powerscourt Centre, South William Street (near Coppinger Row; Creative Quarter), +353 1 707 1610, thepepperpot.ie open daily

### WALL & KEOGH
45 South Richmond Street (near Lennox Street; Portobello)
+353 1 475 9052, wallandkeogh.wixsite.com
open daily

From simple tea and cake service to full-on tea ceremonies and posh five-star experiences, it's safe to say that Dublin's got its tea game firmly sorted.

**Wall & Keogh** lays on quite the spread: the 150-variety-strong menu is as eclectic as the décor, there are gluten-free cake options, plus freshly prepared gimbap (Korean rice rolls). You can't go wrong with the Darjeeling blend and homemade rocky road slices, though.

The black caddies and Art-Deco chandeliers might lend an air of decadence, but it's the carefully selected global teas that really elevate **Clement & Pekoe**. There's no formal afternoon tea menu, but there's nothing to stop you from throwing a little party of your own – the gorgeous, freshly baked scones complement just about any of the teas, though I love the green blend.

**Tea Garden** is a tranquil refuge from traffic-chocked Ormond Quay that offers a tea ceremony experience. Slip off your shoes, find a spot on the floor and get comfy. Friendly staff will offer expert advice about the menu, which features teas from Japan, to India, South America to Turkey. The music and indoor garden will have you in a Zen-like state in no time.

Oven-warm scones, glossy pastries and fantastical pile-'em-high cupcakes have seen **Queen of Tarts** live up to its name. If you're dropping by for tea, be sure to team it with one of the signature plum tarts – you won't regret it.

For a good, old-fashioned milk-and-two-sugars brew and a wedge of award-winning cake, pop into **The Pepper Pot**. Choose from scones with jam, flourless chocolate cake and spicy carrot cake, all within a setting as sweet as the confections themselves.

Looking for something more extravagant? Book in at **The Merrion Hotel**'s "Art Tea". Served in the elegant drawing rooms of the five-star hotel, beverage recommendations come courtesy of the in-house tea masters, but my pick is the jasmine pearl: the leaves are rolled by hand without breaking the veins. What's more, each sweet treat on the menu represents a work of art by an Irish artist. They're so beautiful, it seems almost wrong to eat them. Almost.

With 250 varietals as well as a mouthwatering menu of dainty sandwiches and decadent confections, the afternoon offering at **Oolong Flower Power** is Mad Hatter-worthy. Darjeeling and Earl Grey are perfect accompaniments, but add a glass of Champagne or prosecco to the proceedings and you can easily fall down the rabbit hole and make an evening of it.

# camden quarter

## portobello

— ◆ —

Once known as "Little Jerusalem," the Camden Quarter has long been a melting pot of cultures, ideas and creativity. Back in the 19th century, it was home to this city's Jewish community, and was also the birthplace of Irish playwright and author George Bernard Shaw. Today the neighborhood boasts a diverse mix of cuisine, upmarket brunch spots, quirky open-air arts spaces, awesome pubs and even better live music venues. On a sunny summer's evening, there's nowhere I'd rather be than on the banks of the canal in Portobello, soaking up the last of the sunshine – along with half of this neighborhood's residents.

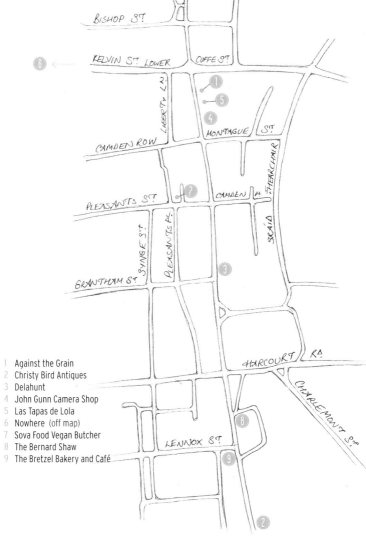

BISHOP ST.

KELVIN ST. LOWER    COFFE ST.

LIBERTY LN

CAMDEN ROW

MONTAGUE ST.

PLEASANTS ST.

SYNGE ST.    PLEASANTS PL.    CAMDEN PL.    SKIÁID FHEARCHAIR

GRANTHAM ST.

HARCOURT RD.

CHARLEMONT ST.

LENNOX ST.

1   Against the Grain
2   Christy Bird Antiques
3   Delahunt
4   John Gunn Camera Shop
5   Las Tapas de Lola
6   Nowhere  (off map)
7   Sova Food Vegan Butcher
8   The Bernard Shaw
9   The Bretzel Bakery and Café

# AGAINST THE GRAIN

*Craft beer emporium*

**11 Wexford Street (at Protestant Row)** / **+353 1 470 5100**
**galwaybaybrewery.com/againstthegrain** / **Open daily**

This cozy, no-nonsense craft brew pub has a vast and ever-changing menu of lagers, ales and IPAs, from the likes of London's Beavertown, Scotland's BrewDog, California's Sierra Nevada and Ireland's own Galway Bay Brewery. The food menu doesn't disappoint either, with juicy burgers, fried chicken wings and delicious chunky chips providing all the sustenance you could need for a night on the beer. Oh, and if you've ever wondered whether pints really do kill brain cells, you can put the theory to the test in their monthly pub quiz, Against the Brain, which takes place on the last Monday of the month.

# CHRISTY BIRD ANTIQUES

*Portobello's treasure chest*

**2 South Richmond Street (near Charlemont Mall) / +353 1 475 4049**
**christybird.com / Closed Sunday**

The pavement outside this old curiosity shop is one of my favorite things about Portobello. For as long as I can remember, it's been a beautiful mess of old-school clocks and garden furniture, bronze figures and retro advertising signs. The original Christy Bird died in 1975, but his legacy lives on through his grandson Christy Bird Flanagan, who continues to fill the shop with gems old and new. Eye-candy comes in the form of Georgian-style doll houses, 1920s travel trunks, vintage lamps, as well as made-to-order furniture. Well worth a gander, especially when they're holding a sale.

# DELAHUNT

*Astounding Irish cuisine with cocktail bar upstairs*

**39 Lower Camden Street (near Grantham Street) / +353 1 598 4880**
**delahunt.ie / Closed Sunday and Monday**

In Victorian times, Delahunt was a greengrocers shop. The pride of Camden Street, it was a purveyor of fine whiskies, teas and turkeys and was even name-checked in James Joyce's Ulysses. Lovingly restored by its current owner Darren Free, Delahunt is now an elegant restaurant brimming with vintage charm - lace curtains, fireplaces, a reclaimed snug and marble table tops. Lunch and dinner menus celebrate seasonal Irish ingredients: think organic Kilkenny Chicken, cheese from Sheridan's (see pg 102) and locally caught seafood. The cocktail bar upstairs is also a lovely spot for pre-dinner drinks. A must-try is their Delahunt G&T – made with Japanese plum wine and Tanqueray gin, it's a fruity take on an old classic.

# JOHN GUNN CAMERA SHOP

*Lights, camera, action!*

16 Wexford Street (near Protestant Row)   +353 1478 1226
johngunn.ie / Closed Sunday

File this one under "endangered species". In a world of Instagram, Photoshop and DSLRs, shops like John Gunn's are a dying breed. Open since 1970, this family-run business specializes in developing black and white photography via their in-house photo lab where they stock specialist film, as well as hard to-find dark room and studio equipment as well as accessories for fine art processing at extremely reasonable prices. Looking for advice? John and his daughters really know their stuff when it comes to all things analog and digital. Drop in for a browse and a chat while you're in the neighborhood.

# LAS TAPAS DE LOLA

*Authentic pinchos*

**12 Wexford Street (at Protestant Row) /** +353 1 424 4100
lastapasdelola.com / **Open daily**

Co-owned by Dubliner Vanessa and Barcelona native Anna, Las Tapas de Lola is one of the Irish capital's most authentic Spanish restaurants. As soon as you step inside, green metro tiles, black-and-white photos and bistro-style chairs transport you to Barcelona. Then there's the menu: it delivers all kinds of yumminess including berenjenas fritas (fried eggplant with maple syrup), bomba de la Barcelona (a huge, breaded, spicy meatball) and my personal pick, the incredible churros con chocolate. Planning a visit? Be sure to reserve a table – I've never seen this place not busy.

# NOWHERE

*For GQ subscribers*

**65 Aungier Street (near Bow Lane East) / +353 1 607 8983
nowhere.ie / Closed Sunday**

Question: Where does the fashion-forward, man-about-town go in Dublin when he wants to update his wardrobe? Answer: Nowhere. Set in a building that dates back to the 1600s, Nowhere stocks lesser-known labels, including Irish designer Alan Taylor and Japanese brand Porter. Run by Swedish-born David Fxiron, the store is gallery-like in look and feel, featuring aluminum fittings, polished concrete and lots of glass. They've recently introduced a range of footwear to their collection including exclusives by Adidas x Raf Simons, Eytys and Novesta, giving gents even more reason to visit.

# SOVA VEGAN BUTCHER

*Tasty meat-free eats*

51 Pleasants Street (near Pleasants Place) / +353 1 85 727 7509
facebook.com/SovaVeganButcher
**Closed Monday and Tuesday**

Okay, so, "vegan butcher" might be something of an oxymoron, but this café is nothing short of genius. Originally from Poland, owner Bart Sova started out by selling yummy vegan meals in pop-ups and market stalls around town. Now a fully fledged brick and mortar, Sova Vegan Butcher serves up healthy brunches, lunches and dinners, all without animal products. The staff are all super friendly and the décor is minimalist but cozy. And the menu? It's both clever and creative – try the chia burger served with house-fermented cucumber and a chunky slaw, and the heavenly chocolate brownie. You'll swear they're too good to be wholesome.

# THE BERNARD SHAW

*Quirky bar and beer garden*

**11–12 Richmond Street South (near Lennox Street) / +353 1 906 2018**
**thebernardshaw.com / Open daily**

Pub. Outdoor gallery. Mini food festival. The Bernard Shaw is many things to many people. It's one of Dublin's most unique drinking establishments, as it hosts weekly Saturday markets as well as the awesome Eatyard, where you can sample a mouthwatering mix of street food delights from vendors including Box Burgers, No Bones Chicken Cones and Veginity (for the veggie-lovers among us), every Thursday through Sunday. Inside, the atmosphere is always electric, but the best craic is to be found out back in the fairy-lit beer garden where it's eternally carnival season. The pièce de résistance is the big blue bus, an old double-decker where you can eat pizza slices on the top deck. Magic.

# THE BRETZEL
# BAKERY AND CAFÉ

*Jewish bread basket*

**1A Lennox Street (at Richmond Row) / +353 1 475 9445**
**bretzel.ie / Open daily**

Easily Dublin's oldest ethnic eatery, Portobello's Bretzel Bakery has been
producing loaves and cakes since 1870. The bakery is certified kosher, and the
handmade, all-butter croissants and pastries are melt-in-the-mouth delish.
The adjoining café is simple but comfortable, and you'll find it perennially
packed with locals. For a sit-in lunch, try a slice of their pizza-style focaccia,
or, if the sun is shining, grab one of their homemade bagels to take away and
enjoy on the banks of the Grand Canal.

# DUBLIN AFTER DARK:
## craft cocktails

*Kindred spirits*

Rule number one of **Vintage Cocktail Club**: ring the doorbell and wait to be invited inside. Rule number two: savor every second in this 1920s-inspired speakeasy, from the oriental décor of the ground floor to the pretty artisan tipples and cozy upstairs surroundings.The cocktail menu is vast, spanning some 600 years of history that covers everything from absinthe to whiskey to sweet vermouth, but I love the Daily Mule, a refreshing mix of vodka, citrus, fruit liqueur, ginger beer, soda and mint.

In the subterranean labyrinth that is **The Liquor Rooms**, the libations are as strong as their famous namesakes. Each of the options on the bar's "cróga" (meaning "brave") menu commemorates a spirited woman from Irish history. Get the party started with the Lola Montez, a heady mix of Absolut Elyx, Aperol, forest fruit tea and hibiscus syrup, before promptly cutting a rug in celebration of this 19th century Irish dancer, actress and mistress of King Ludwig I of Bavaria.

Over in the Grafton Quarter, former wigmaker's shop **Peruke and Periwig** is the place to let your hair down with an expertly crafted drink. Rich mahogany, sleek marble and sumptuous velvet furnishings evoke the elegant grandeur of a by-gone era, while signature ingredients such as elderflower, frangelico, spicy chili sugar and sweet rose water transport you to exotic locales. Blow away the cobwebs with the Kismet, an espresso Martini-inspired extravaganza of vanilla vodka, Kahlua, coffee, caramel and chocolate bitters.

Served in a tall glass with elderflower liqueur, coriander and rhubarb leaves, **Bow Lane's** Gin 'n' Ton Ton might just be the prettiest, most delicious gin and tonic in all of Dublin. Pull up a stool at the ambient oak bar or kick back in one of the luxurious leather banquettes. On the weekends, DJs take to the decks from 9:30pm.

It may not be the same **Chelsea Drugstore** that Mick Jagger sings about in "You Can't Always Get What You Want," but there's plenty of rock 'n' roll edge to this George's Street bar. Think exposed brick, leather button-backed sofas and a soundtrack of soul, funk and 1960s mod classics. Tipples are both bold and beautiful, not least the vodka and prosecco-laced Disco Balls, a drink with as much sparkle as the dazzling signage out front.

### BOW LANE
17 Aungier Street (near East Bow Lane; Camden Quarter) +353 1 478 9489, bowlane.ie, open daily

### PERUKE AND PERIWIG
31 Dawson Street (near Joshua Lane; Grafton Quarter) +353 1 672 7190, peruke.ie, open daily

### THE CHELSEA DRUGSTORE
25 South Great George's Street (near Fade Street; Creative Quarter), +353 1 613 9093 thechelseadrugstore.ie, open daily

### THE LIQUOR ROOMS
5 Wellington Quay (near Parliament Street; Temple Bar), +353 1 339 3688, theliquorrooms.com, open daily

### VINTAGE COCKTAIL CLUB
15 Crown Alley (near Cope Street; Temple Bar) + 353 1 675 3547, vintagecocktailclub.com, open daily

BOW LANE

VINTAGE COCKTAIL CLUB

# DUBLIN AFTER DARK:
## sounds of the city

*Rhythm of the night*

From thumping trad sessions to grungy live gigs, let Dublin's eclectic music scene be your soundtrack to the city.

Whether you're here to catch a live gig in the basement, crash a specialty music night (punk, ska, indie or rockabilly anyone?) or you just want to sample a selection of Dublin's finest craft beer and whiskey in chill surroundings, you'll find all that and more in **The Thomas House**, a happy little dive bar located in the heart of The Liberties.

**Whelan's** has been staging some of Ireland's smallest "big" gigs since 1989. To this day, its cozy spit-and-sawdust vibe continues to draw the likes of Ed Sheeran, Nick Cave and Glen Hansard. With a weekly line-up of mostly homegrown talent, you can experience music from just about every genre here including folk, alternative rock and traditional. Special shout out to the front bar and its toasty turf fire in winter.

Officially Ireland's oldest pub (it dates back to 1198), **The Brazen Head** hosts nightly traditional music sessions as well as open-mic afternoons on Sundays, when audience members are free to join the band on stage for a song. This is a popular venue year-round, but on a summer's evening, the beer garden out front is the perfect spot to sink a pint.

If you're looking for more trad action, swing by **O'Donoghues**. Best known for being the birthplace of legendary Irish folk band, The Dubliners, you'll find this pub always buzzing with an even mix of locals and visitors. I like it for its never-been-messed-with 1960s décor (original low couches and black-and-white photos) as well as its heated beer garden. Never change.

Heading east to Wellington Quay, right next door to the U2-owned Clarence Hotel, you'll find **The Workman's Club.** This retro-themed, multi-level venue is home to some of Dublin's best acoustic sessions, DJ sets and floor-shaking new band nights. Good times guaranteed.

Cavernous and colorful, **The Grand Social** houses four separate event spaces under one roof. My fave section by far is the circus-themed loft, a beautiful, boho live music venue where glowing lightbulbs and a tented ceiling conjure up magical summer festival vibes. On the weekends, expect regular electro, indie, soul and ska club nights in The Ballroom with free admission.

Paraphrasing the famous line by Dublin writer Brendan Behan, **The Cobblestone** likes to think of itself as a "drinking pub with a music problem". Located in the heart of Smithfield, the pub plays host to live music sessions from the early evening on weekdays and from 2pm on weekends. Run by Tom Mulligan, whose family has been playing music for five generations, this is a true Dublin treasure and one of the best places in the city to connect with authentic Irish culture.

### O'DONOGHUES
15 Merrion Row (near Ely Place; Georgian Dublin)
+ 353 1 660 7194, odonoghues.ie, open daily

### THE BRAZEN HEAD
20 Lower Bridge Street (near Usher's Quay;
Temple Bar), + 353 1 677 9549, brazenhead.com
open daily

### THE COBBLESTONE
77 North King Street (at Red Crown Lane; Dublin 7)
+353 1 872 1799, cobblestonepub.ie, open daily

### THE GRAND SOCIAL
35 Lower Liffey Street (near Stand Street Great;
North Quay), +353 1 874 0076, thegrandsocial.ie
open daily

### THE THOMAS HOUSE
86 Thomas Street (at John Street West; The Liberties)
+353 85 203 9047, facebook.com/thomashousedublin
open daily

### THE WORKMAN'S CLUB
10 Wellington Quay (near Parliament Street;
Temple Bar), +353 1 670 6692, theworkmansclub.com
open daily

### WHELAN'S
25 Wexford Street (near Camden Row; Camden Quarter)
+353 1 478 0766, whelanslive.com, open daily

# the grafton quarter

Comprised of Trinity College, the iconic Molly Malone statue and one of Europe's best shopping streets, The Grafton Quarter offers attractions and distractions in abundance. At its core is Grafton Street, an open-air stage for street performers and a retail wonderland of high-street chains and designer labels, as well as luxury department store Brown Thomas and the glass-domed St Stephen's Green Shopping Centre. Venture slightly off-piste, away from the hustle and bustle of the main drag and you're privy to a whole host of charming, character-filled boutiques, restaurants and bars. I love this part of town for its mix of new arrivals and old reliables. Go wander, you'll be justly rewarded.

1 DesignYard
2 Dolce Siciliy
3 Mary's Bar and Hardware
4 Rhinestones (off map)
5 Sheridan's Cheesemongers
6 The International Bar (off map)

# DESIGNYARD

*Contemporary jewelry, sculptures and art*

**25 South Frederick Street (near Nassau Street)** / **+353 1 474 1011**
designyardgallery.com / Closed Sundays

Located in a handsome Georgian building, DesignYard is an emporium of beautifully designed sculptures, jewelry and objets d'art, created by established and up-and-coming designers, including Andrew Geoghegan, Eily O'Connell and Rionore & Co. If you've any sort of weakness for shiny things, you'll love the delicate necklaces and statement gemstone earrings. One of my favorite pieces is a small, sterling silver wing-shaped pendant that I picked up in here a few years ago by German designer Jana Reinhardt. Each time I wear it, I'm reminded of flying, travel and adventures.

# DOLCE SICILY

*Sweet Sicilian treats*

**43 Dawson Street (near South Anne Street)** / **+353 86 840 7360**
facebook.com/theoriginalitalianpastry / Open daily

With its glorious sunshine, movie-set looks and divine cakes and pastries, the island of Sicily had me at "ciao". The good news is I don't have to fly all the way to Palermo whenever I fancy a sweet taste of the Mediterranean island. Dolce Sicily is a lovely, authentic café that serves a delicious range of homemade goodies, including incredible cannoli. Inside, country cottage-style décor – think pastel walls and painted chairs – brings nonna's kitchen to Dawson Street, while outside, the small terrace makes for an ideal spot to enjoy an al fresco coffee. Try a frothy cappuccino and the pistachio cannoli; you won't be disappointed.

# MARY'S BAR
# AND HARDWARE

*Burgers, pints and DIY*

**8 Wicklow Street (near Clarendon Street) / +353 1 670 8629**
**marysbar.ie / Open daily**

Something of a newbie to the Dublin pub scene, Mary's has done its best to stand out from the crowd by resurrecting the old tradition of the pub shop. Back in the day, no country pub was complete without a small grocery store behind the bar, stocking everything from bread and tinned goods to confections and cigarettes. At Mary's, the product range is as varied as it gets, covering breakfast cereal, chocolate, cans of baked beans and soup, as well as DIY essentials such as hammers, lightbulbs and screwdrivers — you know, just in case you're running short (or have never before had need of tools but now you really, really do). Peckish? Order one of their famous toasted ham and cheese sandwiches with your pint or pop downstairs to WOWBURGER, which is under the same ownership, for a juicy beef patty sandwiched between a crisp bun and some garlic butter fries.

# RHINESTONES

*For all that glitters*

18 St Andrew's Street (near Trinity Street) / +353 1 679 0759
facebook.com/dssupplies / Open daily

This vintage jewelry store always reminds me of my friend Marie-Claire, who is slightly obsessed with antique bling. When we were college students, we'd rarely pass this shop without stopping to have a look in the window. I love that the trinkets all have a bit of history to them – some of their original costume pieces date back to the 1920s – and that they are well-traveled, too. Many of the earrings, rings and necklaces have come from as far afield as Paris, Venice and the US. A big bonus is that prices aren't as expensive as you'd imagine – vintage keepsakes start from €25 (US$30), but can peak at €2,000 (US$2,250) for precious heirlooms.

# SHERIDANS CHEESEMONGERS

*Cheese, please*

**11 South Anne Street (near Upper Duke Lane)** / **+353 1 679 3143**
**sheridanscheesemongers.com** / **Closed Sundays**

Founded by brothers Kevin and Seamus Sheridan, this fromagerie began life as a market stall in Galway selling Irish and international cheeses. The South Anne Street store has been satisfying Dublin dairy fiends since 1997, with homegrown labels including Cooleeney, a creamy, buttery farmhouse creation from Tipperary; Wicklow Ban, a mild brie; and the semi-firm, nutty Gubbeen from West Cork. Pair any of these with Sheridan's tasty brown bread crackers, add a sunny day and a perch in a park, and you've got the makings of a delicious picnic.

# THE INTERNATIONAL BAR

*Beers and belly laughs*

**23 Wicklow Street (near St Andrew's Street) / +353 1 677 9250**
**international-bar.com / Open daily**

Located on the corner of Wicklow and St Andrew's Streets, The International Bar has been on the go for over 200 years. One of the first things you'll notice is the floor mosaic at the entrance – the family crest of the O'Donoghue family who began running the pub in 1886. The interior is authentically Victorian, with hand-carved mahogany river gods peering out from behind the bar. There's entertainment nightly; catch a comedy gig upstairs or stick around the lounge for live music performances. Tip: if you're planning to watch the comedy, arrive early. The space upstairs is tiny and you may unwittingly become part of the act as the seats up front are on the stage.

# georgian dublin

———— ✦ ————

Filled with what look like elegant, life-sized doll houses,
Georgian Dublin is based around five leafy squares.
The Georgian period lasted from 1714 to 1840 and
takes its name from the four King Georges who ruled
Great Britain and Ireland. It was a time of rapid change
in Dublin, when higgledy-piggledy medieval buildings
and laneways were razed in favor of wide streets,
redbrick townhouses and landscaped parks and gardens.
Nowadays, families are drawn to its museums, galleries
and greenery, while photographers can't get enough of
the brightly painted front doors. I love it for all of the
above, but also for its small restaurants, time capsule
pubs and slightly eccentric shops.

1 Alchemy Juice Co.
2 CoCu
3 Etto
4 HotAir
5 MAKESHOP
6 Sweny's Joycean Pharmacy
7 The Sugar Club
8 Toners

# ALCHEMY JUICE CO.

*Destination detox*

**5 Lower Leeson Street (at Leeson Lane) / +353 1 670 6217**
**alchemyjuice.ie / Closed Sunday**

Whether you're vegan, ketogenic or paleo, healthy eatery Alchemy Juice Co.
certainly doesn't discriminate. Run by sisters Domini and Peaches Kemp,
this one-stop clean-eating shop serves up super nutritious breakfasts,
lunches, juices and snacks. If you're looking for something to help power
you through town, you can't go wrong with a bottle of their cold-pressed,
spinach-rich gateway juice (spinach, romaine, celery, pineapple, apple, pear,
parsley, lemon and ginger), but if you want something to eat, there's the
paleo stew made with a medley of butternut squash, eggplant, cauliflower,
cherry tomatoes, Portobello mushrooms, coconut milk, garlic, chili, ginger
and turmeric.

# COCU

*For goodness sake*

**9 Upper Baggot Street (near Mespil Road)** / **+353 86 130 3319**
**cocu.ie** / **Closed Sunday**

Short for "counter culture," CoCu is a fast food joint with a twist. Forget greasy take-out, this place is all about over-the-counter grub made from local, seasonal and healthy ingredients. Chef Emilia Rowan cares so deeply about the menu that she even consulted with a dietician to ensure everything is nutritionally balanced. For brekkie on the go, grab one of their energy pots packed with granola, yogurt and fresh fruit or plan an al fresco feast around their superfood-laden lunch boxes, which include your choice of a protein (think garlic and chili prawns and pickled beetroot), base (lettuce, rice, sweet potato or slaw) and topping of nuts, seeds and herbs. The falafel served with pickled carrot, cherry tomatoes, cucumber, hummus and tahini dressing is always a good choice.

# ETTO

*Small but perfectly formed wine bar and restaurant*

**18 Merrion Row (near Ely Place) / +353 1 678 8872 / etto.ie
Closed Sunday**

Simple minimalist décor lets the Italian-inspired menu do all the talking at Etto. And boy does the menu have lots of stories to tell. Personally, I'm partial to the spinach and ricotta malfatti dish. Served with delicate porcini mushrooms and sage butter, it's melt-in-the-mouth good. Be sure to leave room for the red wine prunes and vanilla mascarpone dessert too – it's one of the most surprisingly delicious combinations on the menu. The restaurant is small and, thanks to its Michelin Bib Gourmand Award, busy – booking is essential if you want to secure a table for dinner, although walk-ins are welcome at the bar.

# HOTAIR

*Late-night blow-outs*

**67 Mespil Road (near Flemmings Place) / +353 1 563 8300zz**
**hotair.ie / Open daily**

There are two very good reasons for ladies to love HotAir, a hair salon by OSLO Beauty. Firstly, they open much earlier and close much later than most other hair studios in the city. Secondly, they offer a blow dry and hair styling menu, and a very cool one at that. The options are named after different cities around the world: I usually go for the London, which includes loose curls and gives off a "done, but not too done" look, but other options include the sleek, slicked-back Havana, a chic chignon that is – what else? – Paris, a retro-glam take on finger waves dubbed LA, and the Milan, which features bouncy, voluminous curls. If you want to be done-up for a special event, HotAir also offers makeup application and spray tans to complete your whole look. Just add a killer outfit and go.

# MAKESHOP

*Where every day's a school day*

**4 South Leinster Street (near Leinster Lane)** / **+353 1 662 4416**
**dublin.sciencegallery.com/makeshop** / **Closed Sunday**

This educational workshop and toy store is a side project of Trinity College's Science Gallery. With courses in technology, science and coding for all ages, MAKESHOP is doing its bit to secure the future of Dublin's "Silicon Docklands". A range of drop-in classes are open to anyone who stops by: just choose one of the options available, from robot making to building your own clock or FM radio. Classes last from 45 minutes to two hours, with prices starting at €10 (US$12). It's a great rainy day activity that'll help you hone skills or teach you a brand new one.

# SWENY'S JOYCEAN PHARMACY

*Go for the lemon soap, stay for the theatrics*

1 Lincoln Place (near West Merrion Square) / +353 87 713 2157
sweny.ie / Open daily

Sweny's claims to be "Dublin's worst pharmacy". Take their word for it:
this is no chemist and is instead a time machine waiting to transport you
to Edwardian Dublin. Curated by PJ Murphy, Sweny's Pharmacy dates from
1847 and has been preserved to look exactly as it did when Joyce wrote
about it in the Lotus Eaters chapter of *Ulysses*. Well maybe not exactly as it
looked – secondhand books now take the place of pills and potions. They do
however still sell the famous "sweet lemony wax" (read: lemon-scented soap)
mentioned in the tome. Pop in to pick up a bar and you just might be cajoled
into lending your voice to a Joycean reading. You have been warned.

# THE SUGAR CLUB

*Come to the cabaret*

**8 Lower Leeson Street (near Leeson Lane) / +353 1 678 7188**
**thesugarclub.com / Open daily**

The Sugar Club's is one of Dublin's most eclectic nightlife venues. Here, you can sip cocktails, catch a classic movie screening, be entertained by a musical theater performance or experience an intimate live music set ranging in genre from jazz to ska to blues. Formerly the home of The Irish Film Theatre, with the classy, tiered banquette seating to prove it, this is the ideal pick for anyone looking for something a little bit different to do with their evening. The monthly line-ups are always creative and evolving, so be sure to visit their website, or check the billboard on the front of the building for news of what's on.

# TONERS

*Charming Victorian bar and beer garden*

**139 Lower Baggot Street (at Rogers Lane) / +353 1 676 3090
tonerspub.ie / Open daily**

Not only does Toners claim to serve up one of the best pints of Guinness in Dublin, but it's also said to be the only pub in the city to have captured the heart of WB Yeats. Open since 1818, Toners exudes a genteel, Old World charm, retaining many original features including glass cabinets behind the bar and a traditional wooden snug area which has changed little since Victorian times. Out back, there's a surprisingly spacious beer garden — actually, one of my favorites in the city. It's gloriously sunny in the summer months and a lovely heated outdoor space during the rest of the year.

# literary pubs

*For drinkers with writing problems*

### GROGANS
15 South William Street (at Coppinger Row; Creative Quarter), +353 1 677 9320, groganspub.ie, open daily

### KEHOE'S
9 South Anne Street (near Upper Duke Lane; Grafton Quarter), +353 1 677 8312 louisfitzgerald.com/kehoes, open daily

### MCDAIDS
3 Harry Street (near Chatham Lane; Grafton Quarter), +353 1 679 4395, facebook.com/McDaids open daily

### MULLIGAN'S
8 Poolbeg Street (near Tara Street; Docklands) +353 1 677 5582, mulligans.ie, open daily

### THE PALACE BAR
21 Fleet Street (near Westmoerland Street; South Quay), +353 1 671 7388, thepalacebardublin.com open daily

MULLIGAN'S

In the same way Parisian writers have their cafés, so too,
Dublin writers have their pubs.

Although open since 1899, literary-wise **Grogans** only really hit its stride
in the 1970s, when barman Paddy O' Brien, moved here from another pub,
bringing many of his best customers and wordsmiths with him. No doubt,
Grogans' no music, no television policy did much to encourage conversation
and banter among its clientele. To this day, the pub still attracts a bohemian
set and is easily one of Dublin's friendliest watering holes. The lively outdoor
terrace is one of my favorite things about South William Street.

Fleet Street's **The Palace Bar** has been a favorite with writers since 1843,
counting notorious barflies Brendan Behan and Patrick Kavanagh amongst its
most well-known customers. Over the years, the pub also fostered strong ties
with *Irish Times* journalists, most notably during the 1930s and '40s when the
editor, Robert M. Smilie, held regular literary gatherings here. He and his team
regularly took over the pub's snug and back room, treating the space (and its
telephone box) as an unofficial office.

Meanwhile, in the Grafton Quarter, **Kehoe's** of South Anne Street was one of
Samuel Beckett's haunts. Kehoe's made a name for itself as a literary hangout
in the 1940s and 1950s, but these days it draws a steady mix of tourists and
after-work crowds. On a sunny summer's evening, you'll be lucky to find elbow
room on the pavement outside.

Another firm favorite with the literary set of yesteryear, **McDaids** is a small
narrow pub, with plenty of Victorian character. Seats are hard to come by on
weekends, when much of the crowd flows out onto Harry Street.  Visit on a
weekday afternoon if you want to savor the surroundings over a quiet pint.

Mentioned in James Joyce's short story, *Counterparts*, **Mulligan's** has been a
hit with writers and journalists since it opened its doors on Poolbeg Street in
1854. A little known John F. Kennedy even dropped in for a pint in
this fine Victorian establishment when he worked as a journalist for
Hearst newspapers in the 1950s.

# docklands

Known affectionately as the "Silicon Docks," this neighborhood – which stretches from the North Quays to leafy Dublin 4 – is the beating heart of Dublin's tech and financial services sector. Transformed in the late '90s and '00s from a down-at-heel, derelict wasteland, into the home of some of the city's most visually exciting feats of engineering and architecture, the most striking of which include the Samuel Beckett Bridge, the Convention Centre (aka "the tube in the cube"), the futuristic Bord Gáis Energy Theatre and the Aviva Stadium, a glistening temple to sports. Slick skyscrapers may give the impression that this area is all work and no play, but crack the tough, business-like exterior and you'll discover plenty of interesting finds. You just need to know where to look.

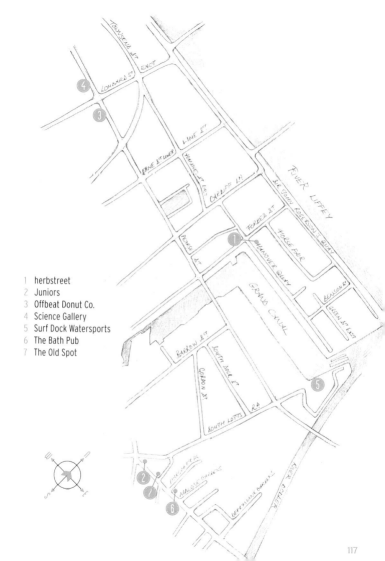

1  herbstreet
2  Juniors
3  Offbeat Donut Co.
4  Science Gallery
5  Surf Dock Watersports
6  The Bath Pub
7  The Old Spot

# HERBSTREET

*Healthy, sustainable eats*

**9 Hanover Quay, Grand Canal Dock (near Asgard Road)**
**+353 1 675 3875 / herbstreet.ie / Open daily**

The early bird catches the worm (or the table) at herbstreet. From breakfast through to lunch and dinner, this is one of the area's busiest restaurants. Once snugly seated, the menu offers plenty of locally sourced, sustainable dishes to mull over, including spicy buffalo wings with Cashel Blue cheese dip, grilled Irish mackerel, 4 oz. steak sandwiches and nutritious salads studded with tabbouleh and goji berries. On weekends, it's a prized brunch spot with queues regularly spilling out onto Hanover Quay. For brunch-time noms, I can never say no to their Eggos Mexicalos, a spicy mound of baked free-range eggs, pinto beans, green onion, tortilla chips and avocado salsa that's well-worth the wait.

# JUNIORS

*New York-style deli by day, Italian restaurant by night*

**2 Bath Avenue (near Shelbourne Road) / +353 1 664 3648**
**juniors.ie / Open daily**

Run by brothers Paul and Barry McNerney, Juniors likes to think big. During the day, expect thickly-cut pastrami sandwiches with all the trimmings, but when night falls, this dynamic eatery is a top pick with weekday office workers, weekend sports fans (as well as rugby players!) en route to or from the Aviva Stadium, and, well, me. I love everything about the supper menu, especially the rustic seafood stew and clam linguini. Plus, I strongly suggest leaving room for dessert — the baked vanilla cheesecake is out of this world.

# OFFBEAT DONUT CO.

*Wonderfully weird doughnuts*

**Pearse Station, 2 Westland Row (near Pearse Street) / +353 1 670 6164**
**offbeatdonuts.com / Open daily**

At Offbeat Donut Co. it's a bit like your favorite sugar-coated treat got together with a humble doughnut and had a sweet little baby. From apple crumble to lemon meringue, crème brûlée, black forest and s'mores, choosing just one flavor can be a bit bewildering; so go for two, or even three. These confections are made slightly smaller than the average doughy offering, so there's no need to feel guilty – or that's what I tell myself, anyway. If I had to pick just one, though, it would be the Ferrero Rocher. Not only is it coated in Nutella and toasted hazelnuts, but it comes with a whole Ferrero Rocher chocolate inside. Seriously dreamy.

# SCIENCE GALLERY

*Where science and art collide*

**The Naughton Institute, Pearse Street (near Westland Row)**
**+353 1 896 4091 / dublin.sciencegallery.com / Closed Monday**

In 2008, Trinity College took a chance on fusing the worlds of science and art. The result is Science Gallery, one of the city's most unique museum experiences. Look forward to thought-provoking exhibitions on how science and technology can complement the creative process for music, art and crafts, as well as fascinating shows on the impact of artificial intelligence. Admission is free and it's highly interactive – there are heaps of experiments to try. During recent exhibit *Sound Check*, visitors explored the intersection of recycling and music by inventing new instruments and sounds. If you fancy having a go at something a bit more complex, head over to their MAKESHOP (pg 110) and get to grips with building a mini robot or FM radio.

# SURF DOCK WATERSPORTS

*Watersports school and surf shop*

**Grand Canal Dockyard (near Bridge Street) / +353 1 668 3945**
**surfdock.ie / Closed Monday and Tuesday**

All work and no play makes Jack a dull boy. Fortunately, the guys at Surf Dock Watersports are on hand to inject a little adrenaline-fueled fun into our downtime. Established in 1992, the guys here have been on the go ever since, offering lessons in windsurfing, kayaking, stand-up paddle boarding, wake boarding, sailing and even SUP yoga and dragon-boating. Introductory classes take place in the sheltered, flat water confines of the Grand Canal Basin and can be booked by phone or via their website. Although all watersports gear can be rented on-site, their shop also stocks a wide selection of wetsuits, surfboards, clothing and other accessories.

# THE BATH PUB

*Cocktails, craft beer and rugby*

**26 Bath Avenue (at Margaret Place)** / **+353 87 762 8039**
**bathpub.ie** / **Open daily**

Located in the shadow of Aviva Stadium, The Bath Pub is a great spot to
soak up the pre- or post-match atmosphere during the big game. In the
summertime, or any day when the weather gods are playing ball, the beer
garden out front is a little sun trap. Fancy a change from the black stuff?
Sample their craft beer menu or push the boat out (aka, splurge) with a
tipsy tea party where the gin cocktails are served in quirky, vintage-style
teapots. On a lazy summer's afternoon, I'm partial to a drop of Elderflower
Collins (gin, elderflower syrup, lemon juice and soda water) or a glass of their
delicious Pimm's.

# THE OLD SPOT

*Cozy gastropub*

**14 Bath Avenue (at Bath Avenue Place)** / **+353 1 660 5599**
theoldspot.ie / Open daily

With its exposed brick, snug leather banquettes and vintage ink drawings,
décor-wise, The Old Spot does its best to live up to its name. But lovely as the
surroundings are, it's the food that takes center stage. The gastropub menu,
including dry-aged ribeye, salt marsh duck and a gussied-up cheeseburger,
has won justly deserved plaudits from all over town, and even impressed
the Michelin folks. I wholeheartedly recommend their Sunday lunch. Full of
flavor, their juicy roast chicken comes served with duck fat roasted potatoes,
roasted root vegetables and creamy cauliflower cheese. Always tastes
like more.

# parks and gardens galore

*Verdant, open spaces*

### BLESSINGTON STREET BASIN
Blessington Street (near Primrose Street;
Phibsborough), +353 1 222 5278, dublincity.ie
open daily

### FITZWILLIAM SQUARE
Fitzwilliam Square (near Pembroke Lane; Georgian
Dublin), no phone, dublincity.ie, open daily

### IVEAGH GARDENS
Clonmel Street (near Sráid Fhearchair; Camden
Quarter), +353 1 475 7816, iveaghgardens.ie
open daily

### MERRION SQUARE
Merrion Square (near Lower Mount Street; Georgian
Dublin), +353 1 222 5278, dublincity.ie, open daily

### PHOENIX PARK
Phoenix Park (near Chesterfield Avenue;
Kilmainham), +353 1 820 5800, phoenixpark.ie
open daily

### ST STEPHEN'S GREEN PARK
St Stephen's Green Square (between Earlsfort
Terrace and Sráid Fhearchair; Georgian Dublin)
+353 1 475 7816, ststephensgreenpark.ie, open daily

No matter the season, Dublin's park life awaits. If it's summer, grab your shades and a syrupy 99, but even if the weather is dreary and gray, you can bundle up and still enjoy a nice, brisk walk, basking in the elements.

Tucked behind a gate just off Harcourt Street, **Iveagh Gardens** is my favorite park in the city. Not only is it extraordinarily pretty with its cascading waterfall and rose gardens, but it's also become an events space, regularly hosting small summer concerts and gigs, as well as the annual Taste of Dublin food festival.

Just a stone's throw from the National Gallery of Ireland, **Merrion Square** was once a private garden, only accessible to key holders from the surrounding Georgian homes. Nowadays, everyone can enjoy this beautiful, landscaped space under the watchful eye of Oscar Wilde, whose statue reclines on a boulder of white quartz. At the weekend, don't miss the Sunday open-air art exhibitions that take place year-round.

ST STEPHEN'S GREEN

There's no mistaking **St Stephen's Green Park**. This 22-acre green lung is a true landmark as well as a giant playground for adults and little ones alike. Feed the ducks and swans on the lake, tackle the swings, slides and roundabouts, and discover the sensory garden's aromatic herbs and shrubs.

The sprawling **Phoenix Park** is twice the size of New York's Central Park and is one of the largest green spaces in Europe. Originally a royal hunting park, it's home to wildlife galore, most famously a herd of fallow deer, descendants of the originals introduced in the 1660s. These days, the park is a paradise for runners, walkers and cyclists. If you want to get in on the action, bring your trainers or rent a bike from the Parkgate Street entrance.

Phibsboro's **Blessington Street Basin** is a hidden gem of a park. Enter the former reservoir through the gateway in the stone wall to fully experience the glorious sight of the plants and trees unfolding like an urban oasis. This park is a lovely quiet place to stroll or sit with a book and enjoy.

From May to September, there's no better place to picnic than **Fitzwilliam Square**. Over the summer months, the Thursday street food market rolls into this lovely Georgian park, bringing with it live music and tasty lunch from a range of gourmet vendors. When the weather's especially beaut, the park is no stranger to hosting outdoor cinema screenings, so be sure to check their social media to see what's on while you're in town.

MERRION SQUARE